TICKED OFF & THRIVING

ALPHA-GAL-FRIENDLY RECIPES THAT DON'T MISS THE MOO

BY SABRA STONE

Ticked Off & Thriving: Alpha-Gal-Friendly Recipes That Don't Miss the Moo
Copyright 2026 by Sabra Stone
All rights reserved. No portion of this book may be reproduced, stored in a retrieval system, or transmitted in any form or by any means—electronic, mechanical, photocopy, recording, scanning, or other—except for brief quotations for review or citing purposes, without the prior written permission of the author.
Published by Argyle Fox Publishing | argylefoxpublishing.com
ISBN 979-8-89124-199-2

So, you got bit by a tick and now you can't eat beef.

Welcome to the club. No one asked to join, but we're here, and we're thriving.

I've lived with Alpha-Gal Syndrome (AGS for those in the know) since 2012. Over the years, I've taken chances, almost died a few times, and felt sorry for myself. Eventually, I even made peace with my new life.

This cookbook is the result of my decision to make the best of a situation that really bites. It's written for everyone who misses their favorite meals due to a blood-sucking tick. Whatever meal your taste buds long for, there's probably a work-around in these pages.

Inside, you'll find recipes made for real people who still want comfort food that doesn't taste like dread and misery. I've swapped out mammal meat with emu, ostrich, duck, and alpha-gal-safe pork. (Yes, that is a thing now!) I've tested alternative fats, cleaned up the labels, and magically managed to make food that tastes like a hug.

If you're looking for healthy eating, you're in the wrong place. This isn't a diet book. It's not low-cal. It's not exactly clean eating. It's survival with style. Delicious, safe, and—like me, sometimes hilariously stubborn.

Right away, I'd like to give credit where it's due. Two companies have changed my life and the way I eat since starting my alpha-gal journey.

Amaroo Hills Emu Farm is an all-natural farm with locations in Ashland City, Tennessee, and Liberty, North Carolina. They sell USDA-inspected emu meat and more. I turn to them for ostrich meat, alpha-gal-safe pork, duck, chicken, and more. Soon after I first heard of them in 2015, I visited the farm. I had no idea what emu tasted like at the time. The gracious owners were kind enough to show me around the farm. They even cooked some samples for me to try before buying. After one taste of emu, I was hooked.

Thankfully, you don't have to travel to the farm to pick up your meat. They also ship. Everything I've ever ordered from them has been wonderful, and they're always adding new products. It's great to once again eat meat that tastes like beef, especially as it doesn't have any of the hormones and whatever else the big box stores add.

Check them out at AmarooHills.com, and order some non-beef steak today!

D'Artagnan is another wonderful source for ethically raised, antibiotic- and hormone-free meats. I first found them in 2013, when I was trying to find a place that sold duck bacon. I've been buying from them ever since. The duck bacon is so close to pork bacon you can hardly tell the difference.

In addition, they have delicious poultry, seafood, charcuterie, gifts, collections, and much more! You can find them at DArtagnan.com. Their quality and customer service is amazing. You won't be disappointed. Trust me.

Now, grab your apron, maybe a glass of wine, and join me in flipping off the tick, one recipe at a time.

Welcome to *Ticked Off & Thriving*.

Contents

The Day Everything Changed • 7
Disclaimer • 9
Starters • 11
Mains • 21
Sides • 57
Sweet Treats • 67

The Day Everything Changed

I was sitting behind the front desk at work when it hit me. My head felt light, detached from my body. My heart pounded in my ears. It was like I downed six espresso shots at once. Something was terribly wrong.

I grabbed my things. "I have to go," I explained to a coworker as I rushed out the door to my car. I didn't know what was happening, only that I needed to get home. Every red light seemed to mock me on the thirty-minute drive home.

I must be having a panic attack, I thought. But why? I'd never had one before.

I wondered if it could be something I'd eaten. All I ate that day was an Angus burger combo from Arby's, and that was four hours earlier.

My fingers started to go numb. I shook my hands, trying to wake them up, panic climbing higher. I'm dying, I kept thinking. This is what it's like to die. I think I'm going to die.

Ten miles from home, my hands were practically useless. They rested on the steering wheel, but they didn't have any feeling. Then my feet started tingling. I used every ounce of willpower to keep driving. "Just make it home," I repeated to myself. "John will know what to do."

By the time I turned down our driveway, I could barely feel my hands. I steered with my palms and blew the horn with my elbow. No one moved inside the house.

I dropped my phone trying to call John. My fingers wouldn't work, so I used a knuckle to tap John's name on my Favorites list. "I think I'm dying," I gasped. "I can't feel my hands or feet, and I think I'm hyperventilating."

"I'm on my way!" John promised.

My skin was a hot, burning red, a raging sunburn spreading across my body at will. Cold water. I needed cold water.

I used four cupped fingers to open the car door and tumbled to the ground. My legs had no feeling. I half-crawled, half-rolled into the house. John wasn't home, but he left the door unlocked. I used my palms to twist the handle, then crawled to the bathroom, turned the knob to cold, and fell fully clothed into the tub.

The shock of the icy water jolted me. Drenched and trembling, I focused on my breathing until John burst in. He helped me into a dry robe and onto the bed while I talked to a 911 dispatcher.

What's your emergency?

"I think I'm dying."

What's going on?

"I don't know—I can't breathe. My whole body is red, and I can't feel my hands or feet."

The dispatcher confirmed my address and said help was on the way. I responded by vomiting. Strangely, I felt a little better after my quick upchuck.

Forty-five minutes later, the ambulance arrived. My skin was still bright red, but my breathing had calmed and I was regaining feeling in my limbs.

The EMTs looked me over. One suspected an allergic reaction and shrugged. "Call us if it happens again," he said.

After they left, I thought back to a cookout weeks earlier. I'd gotten unbearably itchy after eating a burger. I picked up my phone and typed beef allergy into Google.

The first thing that popped up gave instant clarity: Allergy to red meat caused by tick bite.

I'd gotten two tick bites a few weeks earlier.

And so, my alpha-gal journey began.

Enough drama already. Let's eat!

Disclaimer

Warning: I'm not a doctor. I'm not pretending to be a doctor. And frankly, most doctors don't even know what Alpha-Gal Syndrome is, let alone how to eat around it.

This cookbook is based on my own experience living with AGS for over a decade, reading labels, surviving every accidental exposure, and figuring out how to make food that doesn't ruin my day (or worse). I tolerate dairy usually, but I've included alternatives for those who don't.

All that to say, you're responsible for your own health and safety.

Always read labels, double-check ingredients, and talk to a trusted medical professional if you're unsure. Ask questions, even if your doctor looks at you like you're describing a fictional condition invented by a TikTok mom in a bonnet. It's fine. We've all been there.

Also, remember that what's safe for me might not be safe for you. I only react to beef and pork. You may have other intolerances and allergies. Work around them. This book is a guide, not gospel.

Now, go forth and eat like the thriving, tick-bitten legend you are.

Starters

The calm before the craving.

Poppin' Jalapeño Dip

Serves: 8   **Prep Time:** 10 min   **Cook Time:** 25 min
Mood: Spicy.

Ingredients
- 2 (8 oz) blocks cream cheese, softened
- 2–3 jalapeños, seeded and diced (leave some seeds for extra heat)
- 4 slices alpha-gal-safe bacon (duck, emu, or alpha-gal-free pork), cooked and crumbled
- ½ tsp garlic powder
- ¼ tsp smoked paprika
- Sprinkle of red pepper flakes (the more, the spicier)
- 2 tbsp fig preserves (pear or peach will work if you can't find fig)

Instructions
1. In a medium-sized pan on medium-low heat, combine cream cheese, jalapeños, red pepper flakes, most of the bacon, garlic powder, paprika, and preserves. Set aside some bacon for topping. Stir until smooth.
2. Let cool slightly, then top with extra bacon crumbles before serving.

Serving Tip: Serve warm with tortilla chips, crackers, or fresh veggie sticks.

Note: I made this one up when I realized I didn't have enough jalapeños for poppers, and it turned out great! It disappeared faster than gossip at a family reunion. Better double it if your crowd likes a kick.

14

Starters

Asparagus Bacon Twists

Serves: 6–8   **Prep Time:** 15 min   **Cook Time: 15 min**
Mood: Pig in the blanket, but bougie.
Tastes: Gooey, crunchy, and savory all in one bite.

Ingredients
- 1 bunch medium-sized asparagus
- 1 can of crescent rolls
- 8 slices alpha-gal-free bacon of your choice (I prefer alpha-gal-free pork bacon from Amaroo Hills for this recipe)
- 1 tbsp olive oil
- Salt and pepper to taste
- Optional: Grated Parmesan
- Optional: Dijon mustard (so good!)

Instructions
1. Preheat oven to 375°F and line a baking sheet with parchment paper.
2. Wrap each asparagus spear with a half slice of bacon.
3. Cut crescent dough into strips and spiral wrap around the bacon-wrapped asparagus.
4. Place on baking sheet. Brush lightly with olive oil, then season with salt and pepper.
5. Bake until bacon is crisp and dough is golden, about 15 minutes.
6. If desired, sprinkle with Parmesan before serving.
7. Dip in Dijon mustard for a little extra zing.

Note: These are always a hit at any gathering, so make plenty!

14

Starters

Butternut Squash Rings with Brie & Pomegranate Arils

Serves: 6   **Prep Time:** 10 min   **Cook Time:** 25 min
Mood: Let's confuse the guests.

Ingredients
- 1 large butternut squash, sliced into 2-inch rings with seeds removed
- Olive oil spray or 2 tbsp olive oil
- Salt and pepper to taste
- 6 small wedges brie cheese
- ½ cup pomegranate arils
- Fresh spinach or arugula for serving
- Optional: Honey or balsamic glaze (for drizzle)

Instructions
1. Preheat oven to 400°F.
2. Brush squash rings with olive oil, season with salt and pepper, and roast on a parchment-lined pan for 20–25 minutes until tender.
3. Place a wedge of brie in the center of each ring and top with pomegranate seeds.
4. Return to oven for 2 minutes, just until the brie softens.
5. Arrange on a bed of greens and drizzle with honey or balsamic glaze, as desired. Add a fresh sprig of thyme on top to make it extra, like you.

Note: Posting a picture of this dish on social will make your childhood bully feel defeated.

16

Starters

Duck, Fig & Goat Cheese Crostini

Serves: 6–8   **Prep Time:** 10 min   **Cook Time:** 10 min
Mood: Bored with the same ol'.

Ingredients
- 1 baguette, sliced into half-inch rounds
- 4 oz goat cheese
- 3 tbsp fig preserves
- 4 strips duck bacon, cooked and chopped
- ¼ cup pecan halves
- Fresh rosemary for garnish

Instructions
1. Preheat oven to 375°F and arrange baguette slices on a baking sheet.
2. Toast 5–7 minutes, just until golden.
3. Spread each slice with goat cheese and a small spoon of fig preserves.
4. Top with duck bacon and a pecan half.
5. Garnish with rosemary and serve warm.

Note: I had no idea how good these would be. The sweet and tangy is such a great pair! Also good on crackers but not as good as a fresh baguette.

Mains

Where the magic happens.

22

Mains

Finally, Steak! Seared Ostrich Steak for the Moo-Free Masses

Serves: 1–2   **Prep Time:** 5 min   **Cook Time:** 6–8 min
Mood: I just want a steak like a normal human. Is that too much to ask?
Tastes: Just like a beef steak!

Ingredients
- 1 (6–8 oz) ostrich fan filet steak
- 1 tbsp duck fat, olive oil, or butter
- 1 tsp coarse sea salt
- ½ tsp cracked black pepper
- ½ tsp garlic powder
- Optional: Fresh rosemary or thyme
- Optional: Montreal steak seasoning (for that "fancy steakhouse" flair)

Instructions
1. Bring the ostrich steak to room temp. Let it sit out for 20–30 minutes. Don't rush it. Cold meat equals tough meat.
2. Season both sides with salt, pepper, and garlic powder. Press it in like you mean it. Add herbs if you're feeling extra. There are some great steak seasonings out there, just check the ingredients.
3. Heat a heavy skillet (cast iron is king) over medium-high heat until it's screaming hot. Add duck fat and let it shimmer. If you can tolerate butter, use it!
4. Sear the steak for 3–4 minutes per side. Don't move it around. Let it get that deep, caramelized crust.
5. Check the steak's internal temperature. 125°F = rare. 130°F = medium-rare (recommended). Anything higher, and you're on your own
6. Remove from heat when reaching desired temperature and rest for 5 minutes under foil.
7. Slice against the grain and serve with potatoes, roasted veggies, or just eat it standing over the stove. No judgment.

Notes: Ostrich is lean, so don't overcook it. Treat it like a filet mignon, not a sirloin. Also, you can swap emu fan filet for ostrich meat for another flavor your alpha-free palate will appreciate.

24

Mains

Ticked Off Ribs (Kinda): BBQ Emu Necks That Don't Moo Around

Serves: 1–2   **Prep Time:** 15 min   **Cook Time:** 2.5–3 hr
Mood: I came here for ribs and revenge.
Tastes: Just like beef BBQ ribs.

Ingredients
- 3–6 emu necks
- 2 tbsp olive oil or duck fat
- 1 tbsp smoked paprika
- 1 tsp garlic powder
- 1 tsp onion powder
- 1 tsp salt
- ½ tsp black pepper
- ½–¾ cup of your favorite alpha-gal-safe BBQ sauce
- Optional: ¼ tsp cayenne (we're mad, so why not?)

Instructions
1. **Prep:** Preheat oven to 300°F. Line a roasting pan or deep baking dish with foil.
2. **Dry the Meat:** Pat emu necks dry with paper towels. Dry meat = better sear.
3. **Mix It Up:** Combine spices, coat each neck in oil, and rub 'em down. Dry rub those necks like you're massaging out all the trauma of giving up pork ribs.
4. **Sear for Flavor:** In a hot skillet or Dutch oven, brown the necks on all sides until you get a good crust (about 5–7 minutes). You can skip this step if you're lazy, but don't blame me.
5. **Bake Low and Slow:** Place necks in your roasting pan, cover tightly with foil or a lid, and bake for 2.5–3 hours. You want fall-off-the-bone tenderness.
6. Final Glaze: **Remove foil, baste or brush with BBQ sauce, and return to oven uncovered** for 20 minutes at 400°F. This helps to caramelize that sticky goodness.
7. **Rest and Serve:** Let meat rest for 10 minutes, then serve hot with napkins, a side of potato salad, and a smug smile.

Notes: Emu necks are wild cards. Sometimes thick, sometimes skinny. Cook to tenderness, not time. They taste like beef short ribs with a side of justice. Oh, and make extra. You'll be mad if you don't.

Sabra Stone

26

Mains

Holy Jalapeño Enchiladas

Serves: 6–8   **Prep Time:** 20 min   **Cook Time:** 30 min
Tastes Like: Some lady in Tennessee went to the Dollar General and came back with something called enchiladas and everyone went with it.

Ingredients
- 1 lb emu, shredded or ground (chicken works great also)
- 1 can Rotel (I like the spicy habanero one, but you do you?)
- 1 can refried beans (El Paso has one without lard)
- 1 box Spanish rice
- 1 jar white queso dip (I like Tostitos brand best)
- 1 cup cheese of your choice (I like sharp cheddar)
- 1 package flour tortillas
- 1 tsp cumin
- 1 tsp garlic powder
- Salt and pepper to taste
- Pickled jalapeño slices for topping
- Optional: Cayenne to taste
- Optional sides: Salsa, guacamole, and tortilla chips

Instructions
1. Preheat oven to 375°F.
2. Cook Spanish rice according to box directions.
3. In a skillet with a little olive oil, brown your meat with cumin, garlic powder, salt, and pepper.
4. When meat is fully cooked, add drained Rotel.
5. Spread refried beans on tortilla, add meat and rice, roll up, and place into a casserole dish.
6. When casserole dish is full, add white queso dip.
7. Top with shredded cheese and jalapeños.
8. Bake 20–25 minutes or until bubbly and golden.
9. Serve with salsa, guac, sour cream, and chips (or cheesecake—whatever brightens your day).

Notes: I literally threw this together one day, and it was everyone's favorite. There are so many variations you can add or subtract from this recipe. For example, you can try red enchilada sauce for a more authentic flavor. Just add what you like and leave out what you don't. Enjoy!

Sabra Stone

28

Not Your Mama's Meat Loaf (Unless Your Mama Cooks Emu, in Which Case…Respect)

Serves: 4–6   **Prep Time:** 15 min   **Cook Time:** 1 hour
Mood: I need comfort food.
Tastes: Better than your mom's.

Ingredients

For the Loaf
- 1½ lbs ground emu
- ½ cup finely chopped onion
- 2 garlic cloves, minced
- 1 egg
- ½ sleeve of Ritz crackers
- ¼ cup ketchup
- 1 tbsp Dijon mustard
- 1 tsp salt
- ½ tsp black pepper
- Optional: Chopped parsley or herbs (for a little razzle-dazzle)

For the Glaze
- ¼ cup ketchup
- 1 tbsp molasses
- 1 tsp Dijon mustard
- Optional: Splash of vinegar (for a tangy top)

Instructions

1. Preheat oven to 375°F. Grease a loaf pan or line a baking sheet with parchment.
2. Mix all loaf ingredients in a large bowl. Get in there with your hands, it's not meat loaf until you squish it.
3. Form into a loaf. Place in pan or shape freeform. Emu is lean, so it won't shrink like beef. What you see is what you get.
4. Mix glaze ingredients and slather half on top.
5. Bake for 40 minutes, then pull it out and add the rest of the glaze. Return to oven for 15–20 more minutes or until internal temp hits 160°F.
6. Let it rest for 10 minutes before slicing. Trust me—this is the difference between meat loaf and crumbly emu meat mess.

Notes: Emu is naturally lean and mild. This recipe builds flavor without drying it out. Wanna make it spicy? Add chopped jalapeños, red pepper flakes, or a dab of BBQ glaze in the mix. If you don't serve this with mashed potatoes, I think you're breaking the law in several states, but you do you.

Sabra Stone

30

Mains

Lasagna, 86 the Moo: Because Cows Aren't Invited to Dinner

Serves: 6–8   **Prep Time:** 25 min   **Cook Time:** 70 min
Mood: I don't care what the scale says today.
Tastes Like: Telling everyone your grandma is from Italy, and they believe you.

Ingredients

Meat Sauce
- 1 lb ground emu or ostrich
- 1 tbsp olive oil
- 1 small onion, diced
- 3 cloves garlic, minced
- 1 jar (24 oz) spaghetti sauce or homemade tomato sauce
- 1 tsp Italian seasoning
- Salt and pepper to taste

Ricotta Layer
- 1 cup ricotta cheese (for a dairy-free substitute, go with Kite Hill almond-based ricotta or homemade cashew ricotta)
- 1 egg
- 1 tbsp fresh or 1 tsp dried parsley

Cheese Options (Choose Your Path)
- 2 cups shredded mozzarella (dairy-free sub: Violife or Daiya mozzarella shreds)
- ½ cup shredded Parmesan (dairy-free sub: follow your heart or try Violife Parmesan-style shreds)

Other Stuff
- 9 boiled lasagna noodles
- Olive oil for greasing the pan

Instructions

1. **Make the Meat Sauce:** In a large skillet, heat olive oil. Add onion and cook until soft. Add garlic and stir for one minute. Toss in the ground meat and cook until browned. Pour in spaghetti sauce and season with Italian seasoning, salt, and pepper. Simmer 10 minutes.
2. **Mix the Ricotta Layer:** In a bowl, stir together ricotta (or alternative), egg, and parsley. Set aside.
3. **Layer It Up:** In a greased 9x13 baking dish, spread a little meat sauce on the bottom. Lay 3 noodles down on top of the sauce, add a layer of ricotta mixture, spoon on meat sauce, and sprinkle Mozzarella and Parmesan (or your cheese dupe). Repeat this layering two more times, ending with sauce and cheese on top.
4. **Bake:** Cover with foil (tent it so it doesn't stick to the cheese) and bake at 375°F for 25 minutes. Remove foil, bake 15 more minutes until golden and bubbly. Let sit 10 minutes before slicing.

Notes: You can assemble this ahead and bake it later. You can even add bell pepper if your mom insists. Want to go next-level? Top with a basil leaf and a side of garlic bread. Finally, ground turkey or ground chicken also work great for this recipe.

Most pork is off-limits to those with Alpha-Gal Syndrome due to the alpha-gal sugar molecule in mammal meat. But Amaroo Hills Farm raises pork that tests non-reactive for alpha-gal in sensitive individuals. When I found out, I ordered all the things and let me tell you, the bacon and pork chops are to die for. Still, consult your doctor and patch-test if needed.

Fried Pork Chops Without the Itch, Say What?

This recipe celebrates that rare, golden unicorn: pork that doesn't fight back.
Serves: 2–4   **Prep Time:** 10 min   **Cook Time:** 15 min
Mood: Southern sass.
Tastes Like: Sunday dinner at your aunt's house.

Ingredients
- 4 alpha-gal-friendly pork chops
- 1 cup buttermilk (or 1 cup unsweetened almond milk with 1 tbsp vinegar for dairy-free)
- 1 cup all-purpose flour
- ½ cup cornstarch (for extra crispiness)
- 1 tsp salt
- ½ tsp black pepper
- ½ tsp garlic powder
- ½ tsp paprika
- ½ tsp onion powder
- Duck fat, emu fat, or alpha-gal-safe lard
- Optional: 1 tsp hot sauce (for added pop)
- Optional: Pinch of cayenne (for heat)

Instructions
1. **Marinate the Chops:** Combine buttermilk and hot sauce in a bowl. Submerge pork chops, cover, and refrigerate for 2–4 hours (or overnight if you've got time and ADHD).
2. **Prepare the Breading:** In a shallow dish, mix the flour, cornstarch, salt, pepper, and spices. Stir like you're about to win the state fair.
3. **Heat the Oil:** In a cast iron skillet (because we're doing this right), add enough duck fat or alpha-gal-safe lard to cover the bottom ¼ to ½ inch deep. Heat to medium-high (around 350°F).
4. **Dredge the Chops:** Pull chops from the marinade, let the excess drip off, then press them into the flour mixture. Flip and press again. That crispy coating won't build itself.
5. **Fry 'Em Up:** Carefully place chops into hot oil. Fry for 4–5 minutes per side or until golden brown and 145°F inside. Don't crowd the pan. Let 'em breathe.
6. **Drain and Rest:** Transfer to a wire rack or paper towels. Let rest for 5 minutes while you pretend to wait patiently.

Note: If you want to use that grease up, make some gravy and add it to some mashed potatoes because we're eating real fried pork chops, and that deserves a celebration.

Chorizo Duck Street Tacos

Spicy. Sassy. Moo-free.
Serves: 4   **Prep Time:** 15 min   **Cook Time:** 10 min
Mood: It's winter, and I want to pretend I'm in Mexico.
Tastes Like: A taco truck just pulled up in your driveway.

Ingredients

Meat
- Ground duck chorizo (Amaroo Hills Farm has the best spicy duck chorizo sausage, perfect for these tacos!)

Tortillas
- Small corn tortillas, lightly pan-fried

Toppings
- Shredded cheese (non-dairy if dairy-sensitive)
- Diced onions
- Chopped tomatoes
- Avocado slices or guac
- Fresh cilantro
- Squeeze of lime
- Jalapeños and anything else you like
- Optional: Dollop of dairy-free sour cream or spicy aioli

Instructions

1. Sauté meat in a skillet until browned and slightly crispy.
2. Lightly pan-fry tortillas.
3. Place meat inside the tortillas, add your favorite toppings, and indulge.

Note: Taco Tuesday just quit being basic. These chorizo duck tacos are so good, you may find yourself dancing in the kitchen with a sombrero.

Sabra Stone

36

Mains

Chopped Steak with Onions & Gravy

It's not a hamburger. It's chopped steak. Act accordingly.
Serves: 4
Prep Time: 10 min
Cook Time: 20 min
Mood: Grateful I'm not allergic to birds.
Tastes: Savory and nostalgic, like your favorite greasy spoon that got replaced by a Taco Bell.

Ingredients
- 1 lb ground emu or ostrich (Amaroo Hills Farms has both)
- 1 egg
- 1/3 cup breadcrumbs (or crushed Ritz crackers)
- 2 tsp Worcestershire sauce
- Salt, pepper, and garlic powder to taste
- 1 large onion, sliced
- 2 tbsp oil or duck fat for frying

Gravy
- 2 tbsp flour
- 2 tbsp fat from the pan (or you can use butter or duck fat)
- 1.5 cups chicken broth (or milk if tolerated)

Instructions
1. Mix ground meat, egg, breadcrumbs, Worcestershire, and seasonings. Form into thick oval patties (like mini meat loafs).
2. Sear patties in a hot skillet with fat until browned on both sides. Remove and set aside.
3. Add sliced onions to the skillet, cook until soft and golden.
4. Sprinkle flour over onions, then stir and cook for 1–2 minutes. Slowly whisk in broth or milk to make gravy.
5. Return patties to skillet. Cover and simmer for 15–20 minutes until cooked through and smothered in that glorious gravy.

Note: Serve over mashed potatoes or rice. Garnish with chopped parsley if you're trying to look like you have your life together.

38

Mains

Reubens Are Back on the Menu!

Who said Reubens were off-limits? Not me. Not anymore. This version gives deli vibes without the EpiPen. Crunchy, melty, tangy, and 100% moo-free.

Serves: 2   **Prep Time:** 10 min   **Cook Time:** 5 min
Mood: Feeling like sauerkraut was made for only this.
Tastes: Rich, tangy, indulgent—like you forgot how much you loved Reubens.

Ingredients
- Thinly sliced emu or ostrich pastrami (Amaroo Hills has both!)
- Sauerkraut, drained
- Swiss cheese (or vegan Swiss or Mozzarella if dairy is a no-go)
- Thousand Island dressing
- Rye or pumpernickel bread
- Butter (or olive oil spread if dairy-free)

Instructions
1. Butter the outside of your bread slices like you mean it.
2. On the inside, layer pastrami, Swiss cheese, sauerkraut, and a hearty smear of dressing.
3. Sandwich that masterpiece and grill on a skillet or press until golden brown and the cheese is melted.
4. Slice, serve, and enjoy like you just got a New York deli sandwich without the ER trip.

Note: The sauerkraut in the glass jar is worth the extra money. Dip your fries in Thousand Island instead of ketchup. You'll thank me later.

Alpha-Gal Safe Pork Shoulder Steak

Serves: 2   **Prep Time:** 5 min   **Cook Time:** 35–40 min
Mood: Craving a steak that won't kill me.
Tastes Like: You forgot how good meat was.

Ingredients
- 1 alpha-gal-safe pork shoulder steak (or emu or ostrich shoulder steak if you're subbing)
- 1 tbsp olive oil or duck fat
- 1 tsp salt
- ½ tsp black pepper
- 1 tsp smoked paprika
- ½ tsp garlic powder
- ½ tsp onion powder
- ½ tsp dried thyme (or 1 tsp fresh, chopped)
- ½ cup chicken broth
- 1 tbsp butter
- 3 garlic cloves, smashed
- Optional: Rosemary, lemon, or apple cider vinegar

Instructions
1. **Season Like You Mean It:** Pat the steak dry (trust me, this matters). Rub it down with olive oil, then coat both sides with salt, pepper, paprika, garlic powder, onion powder, and thyme.
2. **Sear for the Drama:** Heat a cast iron skillet on medium-high until it's angry hot. Drop in the steak and sear 3–4 minutes per side until you get that gorgeous golden crust.
3. **Add the Magic:** Turn the heat to low. Add broth, butter, and smashed garlic cloves to the pan. Top with rosemary if ya want. Let it bubble gently, then cover with a lid.
4. **Slow-Finish to Perfection:** Simmer 25–35 minutes, flipping halfway through the simmer. Stop when the steak is tender and almost fork-friendly but still holds its shape.
5. **Reduce and Shine:** Remove the lid, bump the heat slightly, and let the juices reduce into a glossy, savory pan sauce. Taste and hit it with a splash of apple cider vinegar or lemon if you want it brighter.

42

Mains

Spicy Duck Sausage Tortellini Skillet

Serves: 4–6   **Prep Time:** 10 min   **Cook Time:** 30 min
Mood: Cozy chaos in a Tuscan skillet.
Tastes Like: Alfredo got a wild hair and married a spicy duck.

Ingredients

- 1 lb hot Italian duck sausage (one of my Amaroo Hills favorites)
- 12 oz cheese tortellini, fresh or refrigerated (use dairy-free tortellini if needed or substitute with pasta of your choice)
- 2 tbsp olive oil
- Salt and black pepper to taste
- 1 tsp garlic powder
- 3 tbsp butter (use plant-based butter if dairy-sensitive)
- 3 cloves garlic, minced
- 1 cup heavy cream (substitute with coconut cream or unsweetened oat milk + 1 tsp cornstarch if desired)
- ½ cup chicken broth
- ½ cup grated Parmesan cheese (or dairy-free Parmesan/nutritional yeast)
- 1½ tsp dried basil or ¼ cup fresh basil, sliced thin
- 1 tsp Italian seasoning
- 3 cups fresh spinach
- 2 tbsp sun-dried tomatoes
- 2 tbsp fresh parsley, chopped

Instructions

1. **Cook the Tortellini:** Bring a large pot of salted water to a boil. Cook tortellini until tender. Drain and toss with a drizzle of olive oil to keep from sticking.
2. **Brown the Duck Sausage:** In a large skillet, heat olive oil over medium heat. Add sausage and cook until browned, breaking it up with a spoon. Season with salt, pepper, and garlic powder. Remove from the pan and set aside.
3. **Make the Sauce:** In the same skillet, melt the butter. Add minced garlic and sauté for about a minute, until fragrant. Pour in the cream, broth, Parmesan, basil, and Italian seasoning. Simmer 3–5 minutes until slightly thickened.
4. **Bring It All Together:** Add spinach and sun-dried tomatoes to the sauce; stir until the spinach wilts. Return the sausage and tortellini to the skillet and toss gently to coat everything in that creamy goodness. Taste and adjust seasoning as needed.
5. **Serve and Garnish:** Spoon into bowls, sprinkle with parsley and extra cheese (or nutritional yeast), and serve hot. Bonus points if you add crusty bread to soak up every drop of sauce.

Notes: This one's rich, spicy, and silky. Comfort food without the cow. The duck sausage steals the show, but that hit of basil pulls everything together. Nobody's gonna believe it's alpha-gal friendly.

Duck Bacon Breakfast

Serves: 2   **Prep Time:** 5 min   **Cook Time:** 6–8 min
Mood: Turkey move to the back, duck is riding shotgun.
Tastes: Crispy and savory, like you're gonna have a BLT for lunch.

Ingredients
- Duck bacon (from Amaroo Hills, D'Artagnan, or your go-to alpha-gal-safe source)
- Eggs (cooked your way—scrambled, fried, or whatever gets you through the morning)
- Toast or crispy hash browns (bonus if you fry them in duck fat like a true kitchen rebel)
- Optional: Avocado, fruit, or sautéed veggies

Instructions
1. Fry that duck bacon until it's crispy on the edges but still juicy. Duck bacon has more fat than turkey bacon, so keep an eye on it. It'll go from "yum" to "charred" real quick.
2. Cook your eggs to order.
3. Add toast, hash browns, or whatever carbs your soul is craving.
4. Plate it like a diner queen and snap a pic for Insta likes.

Note: Before I found out about emu and ostrich, I came across a post online about duck bacon from D'Artagnan. I ordered some, and it did not disappoint. I've been ordering from them for years, and their customer service is superb! Amaroo Hills now has duck bacon as well, along with emu bacon and alpha-gal-safe pork bacon. I couldn't be happier about it!

46

Mains

What the Emu Pho Is for Dinner?

Because even your soup deserves to be bougie and beef-free.
Serves: 4   **Prep Time:** 15 min   **Cook Time:** 1 hour
Mood: I've outgrown ramen noodles and am adulting now.
Tastes Like: An exotic vacation in a bowl.

Ingredients

- 1 small emu fan fillet, sliced thinly against the grain
- 1 tbsp olive oil or duck fat
- 1/2 onion, sliced
- 2 garlic cloves, minced
- 2–3 star anise
- 1 tsp grated fresh ginger
- Dash of cayenne pepper
- 4 cups Emu Pho Bone Broth (Amaroo Hills, y'all are legends)
- 4 oz rice vermicelli noodles, cooked
- Salt and pepper to taste
- Optional: 1 tbsp sriracha (strongly encouraged)

Toppings
- Fresh mint
- Bean sprouts
- Lime wedges
- More sriracha (because you're brave)
- Optional: Thinly sliced green onions, jalapeño slices, and hoisin drizzle

Instructions

1. In a large pot, sauté onion, garlic, ginger, sriracha and spices in olive oil or duck fat until fragrant. (Put your star anise in a tea ball infuser so that you can remove it before eating)
2. Pour in 4 cups of emu pho bone broth and simmer on low for about an hour to let the flavors build.
3. Meanwhile, cook rice noodles per package instructions and slice the emu fan fillet paper-thin.
4. When ready to serve, place noodles in a bowl. Lay raw emu slices on top and pour the hot broth directly over the meat. It will cook instantly in the bowl like traditional pho.
5. Load up on mint, bean sprouts, and other toppings and eat like the alpha-gal survivor you are.

Note: If you like it really spicy, add hot pepper of your choice to the tea ball infuser with the star anise. I really like habanero.

Sabra Stone

48

Mains

Ground Emu Stroganoff

Serves: 4–6
Prep Time: 15 min
Cook Time: 45 min
Mood: Family potluck winner of the week.
Tastes: Creamy, beefy, and delicious.

Ingredients
- 1 lb ground emu or ostrich
- 2 tbsp butter (duck fat if you can't tolerate butter)
- 1 medium onion, finely chopped
- 2 cloves garlic, minced
- 8 oz mushrooms, sliced
- 2 tbsp flour (or cornstarch for gluten-free)
- 1 cup chicken broth
- 1 tbsp Worcestershire sauce
- 1 tsp Dijon mustard
- ½ cup sour cream (Greek yogurt if tolerated)
- Salt and pepper to taste
- 8 oz egg noodles
- Fresh parsley for garnish

Instructions
1. Cook noodles according to package directions. Drain and set aside.
2. In a large skillet, melt butter over medium heat. Add onions and garlic and sauté until soft.
3. Add ground emu, season with salt and pepper, and cook until browned.
4. Stir in mushrooms and cook until they release their liquid and start to brown.
5. Sprinkle flour over the mixture, stirring well to coat. Cook 1–2 minutes to get rid of the raw flour taste.
6. Slowly add broth, Worcestershire, and mustard, stirring constantly. Bring to a gentle simmer and let thicken (5–7 minutes).
7. Lower heat and stir in sour cream or Greek yogurt. Don't boil at this point, just warm it through until creamy and silky. Adjust seasoning to taste.
8. Serve over noodles and garnish with parsley.

Note: Emu has a rich, beef-like flavor that shines in this dish. Using duck fat instead of butter adds an even deeper, more old-school stroganoff taste while being safe for those who can't tolerate butter.

50

Mains

Spicy Emu Chili

Listen, I love a big ol' pot of chili as much as the next Southern soul, but kidney beans and beef ain't it anymore. This version hits with ground emu and pinto beans. It's spicy, hearty, and alpha-gal-friendly. Moo who?

Serves: 6 **Prep Time:** 15 min **Cook Time:** 1 hour
Mood: Feeling cute. Might enter a chili cook-off.
Tastes: Bold and spicy, like your cat when you forgot to feed her.

Ingredients
- 1 lb ground emu (or ostrich)
- 1 tbsp olive oil
- 1 medium onion, diced
- 3 garlic cloves, minced
- 1 (15 oz) can diced tomatoes
- 1 (15 oz) can pinto beans, drained
- 4 (16 oz) cans pinto chili beans
- 3 cups water
- 1 small can tomato sauce
- 1 tbsp chili powder
- 1 tsp smoked paprika
- ½ tsp cumin
- ¼ tsp cayenne (adjust to taste)
- Throw in a habanero pepper if you're feeling extra
- Salt and pepper to taste
- Optional toppings: Diced onion, avocado, dairy-free cheese, and cilantro

Instructions
1. In a large pot, heat olive oil over medium heat. Add diced onion and sauté until soft.
2. Add garlic and stir for another 30 seconds.
3. Toss in the ground emu. Cook until browned, breaking up with a spoon.
4. Stir in diced tomatoes, tomato sauce, pinto beans, water, and all spices.
5. Let it simmer on low heat for at least 30 minutes (longer if you've got time—it only gets better).
6. Taste and adjust seasoning. Serve hot with your favorite toppings or cornbread.

Note: If you're not feeling all of that dicing and chopping, a can of Rotel is a quick substitute. I like the spicy habanero version.

Zero Baa Gyros

All the flavor, none of the baa.
Serves: 4   **Prep Time:** 20 min   **Cook Time:** 10 min
Mood: I want a gyro so bad.
Tastes: Zesty, fresh, and tempting you to take seconds.

Ingredients

- 1 lb ostrich or emu steak, any cut
- 1 tbsp olive oil
- ½ tsp dried oregano
- ½ tsp garlic powder
- ½ tsp onion powder
- ¼ tsp cumin
- Salt and pepper to taste
- Pita or flatbread (check ingredients for alpha-gal safety)
- Shredded lettuce
- Diced tomatoes
- Sliced red onions
- Crumbled sheep's milk feta (or your dairy-free alternative of choice)
- Optional: Fresh dill, cucumber slices, or pickled red onion

Tzatziki Sauce

- 1 cup plain Greek yogurt or coconut yogurt
- 1 small cucumber, finely grated and squeezed dry
- 1 tbsp lemon juice
- 1 tsp olive oil
- 1 garlic clove, minced
- 1 tsp fresh dill (or ¼ tsp dried)
- Salt to taste

Instructions

1. Mix tzatziki sauce ingredients in a bowl, then place sauce in refrigerator while you make the meat.
2. Heat olive oil in a skillet over medium-high heat.
3. Add ostrich or emu and cook a little under medium, remove from skillet, cut into thin slices, and add back to the skillet.
4. Stir in oregano, garlic powder, onion powder, cumin, salt, and pepper. Let it sizzle and develop a little crust for extra flavor.
5. Warm the pita or flatbread.
6. Spread tzatziki sauce on your pita or flatbread. Layer with meat, lettuce, tomato, onion, feta (if using), and any extra toppings you desire.

Note: Borderline addictive. Eat responsibly.

Backyard Hibachi

Serves: 4   **Prep Time:** 15 min   **Cook Time:** 15 min
Mood: Feeling like hibachi minus the flaming choo choo onion.

Ingredients
- 1 (6–8 oz) emu or ostrich steak (add chicken, shrimp, or more meat, if desired)
- 2–3 cups day-old cooked rice (cold works best)
- 2 eggs
- 2–3 tbsp olive oil
- 2–3 tbsp soy sauce
- 1 tsp garlic powder
- ½ tsp onion powder
- White pepper to taste
- Zucchini slices, onion, mushrooms, peas, or carrots (however much you have on hand)
- Optional: 2 tbsp butter (if tolerated)

Yummy Sauce (Optional but Recommended)
- ½ cup mayo
- Sriracha to taste
- 1 tbsp ketchup
- 1 tsp sugar
- ½ tsp garlic powder
- Splash of water to thin

Instructions
1. **Make the Sauce:** Mix yummy sauce ingredients and chill. This is optional, but you'll be glad you did. Trust me.
2. **Cook the Meat:** Heat oil in a hot skillet or griddle, then add emu or ostrich sliced thin. Season with garlic powder, onion powder, and white pepper. Sear quickly until just cooked, remove from heat, and set aside.
2. **Scramble the Eggs:** Add a little oil to a separate pan, scramble eggs, and set aside.
3. **Fry the Rice:** Add more oil if needed, then the cold rice. Spread rice out and let it crisp before stirring.
4. **Season:** Add soy sauce and butter (if using). Toss eggs in with rice until evenly coated.
5. **Add Veggies and Meat:** Stir in vegetables and cooked meat and cook just until heated through.
6. **Serve:** Serve hot with yummy sauce on the side or drizzled over the top.

Notes: Day-old rice will give you a restaurant-style texture. This works great on a Blackstone griddle or with cast iron, but a large frying pan will do. Also, if you think rice is hard to cook, I got you. Take equal amounts of rice and water. Boil the water, then add rice and a teaspoon of olive oil. Stir, cover, turn down low, and don't even look at it for 30 minutes. Perfect every time! Opening the lid too early is the killer of perfect rice.

Sides

Because no main should stand alone.

58

One day I was feeling cheap and rebellious and thought, "What if I just cooked the whole damn carrot?" Turns out carrot tops are herbaceous, delicious, and basically free greens.

Side-Eye Dishes

Root Awakening: Sautéed Carrots & Tops

When life gives you carrots, eat the leaves too.
Serves: 4   **Prep Time:** 10 min   **Cook Time:** 15 min
Mood: Thrifty with a twist of What if?
Tastes: Earthy, healthy, like you're the kind of person that gardens, meditates, and pays your bills on time.

Ingredients
- A bunch of fresh garden carrots (with leafy tops still attached)
- 1 tbsp olive oil or duck fat
- 2 garlic cloves, minced
- Salt and pepper to taste
- Optional: Squeeze of lemon, pinch of red pepper flakes, or drizzle of honey if you're feeling fancy

Instructions
1. Wash your carrots and their green, leafy tops. Seriously, get the dirt off or you're eating sediment.
2. Trim and peel the carrots. Chop them however your soul desires: rustic chunks, coins, or diagonally if you're extra.
3. Roughly chop the tops. (Yes, they're edible—think parsley, but with a side of judgment.)
4. Heat olive oil or duck fat in a skillet. Sauté the carrots over medium heat until tender and slightly caramelized. You can also oil, season, and air fry on medium-high for about 30 minutes.
5. Toss in the garlic and chopped tops and cook for another 1–2 minutes until wilted. Season with salt and pepper.
6. Serve warm with an optional lemon squeeze or honey drizzle if you want to confuse your guests in a good way.

Note: You're either gonna love or hate the carrot tops. I love them. Be adventurous and try 'em out.

60

Side-Eye Dishes

Leaf Me Alone Collards: We'll get through this one. Promise.

Nobody under 60 likes collards. I don't even like collards, but you can make these when your grandma visits. The grease makes them tolerable, the vinegar makes them edible, and the attitude makes them authentic. Besides, they're good for you, and your mom will be proud.

Serves: 4–6   **Prep Time:** 10 min   **Cook Time:** 45 min
Mood: Collard seeds came with my seed bundle and took over the garden.
Tastes Like: Your folic acid numbers just jumped through the roof.

Ingredients
- 1 big bunch of fresh collard greens
- 1 tbsp duck fat or alpha-gal-safe lard (from Amaroo Hills)
- 1 small onion, diced
- 2 garlic cloves, minced
- 1 cup chicken broth or water
- Salt and pepper to taste
- Optional: Splash of vinegar or hot sauce
- Optional: Pinch of red pepper flakes (if you're feeling hostile)

Instructions
1. Rinse collards thoroughly—like, really rinse them. There's probably a beetle in there.
2. Remove tough stems, roll up the leaves like a cigar, and slice into strips.
3. In a large pot, melt your duck fat or pork grease over medium heat. Add the onion and cook until translucent.
4. Stir in the garlic for 30 seconds, then throw in the collards.
5. Pour in the broth or water and bring to a simmer. Cover and cook for 30–40 minutes or until tender and not bitter.
6. Season with salt, pepper, and whatever passive-aggressive seasoning you need to survive the day.

Note: All joking aside, these really aren't half bad, and you'll feel extra healthy and proud of yourself for eating them. Added bonus: If you like them, they're extremely easy to grow!

62

Side-Eye Dishes

Don't Be Salty—That's My Job Potato Salad

With green olives, because I said so.
Serves: 6–8   **Prep Time:** 20 min   **Cook Time:** 15 min
Mood: Family cookout on the back deck.
Tastes Like: The 4th of July.

Ingredients
- 2.5–3 lbs potatoes (usually russet or similar)
- ½ cup mayonnaise (or alpha-gal-safe alternative)
- 1 tsp yellow mustard for color and a little zing
- ½ cup diced dill pickles or relish
- ½ cup sliced green olives with pimentos
- 2 boiled eggs, chopped
- ¼ cup finely diced red onion
- Salt and pepper to taste
- Paprika for sprinkling on top like Grandma used to do

Instructions
1. Wash, peel, and chop the potatoes into bite-sized pieces.
2. Boil them in salted water until fork-tender. Don't overcook them into mashed potato territory.
3. While your taters boil, grab a separate bowl. Combine mayo, mustard, pickles, olives, eggs, onion, salt, and pepper.
4. When potatoes are done and cooled, add them to the ingredients you just mixed in a bowl and mix, mix, mix. Hand the spoon to your significant other and ask if it needs more mayo or salt.
5. Chill at least 2 hours before serving. Sprinkle with paprika if you're trying to impress your elders.

Note: This is the potato salad that I've made since I was a teenager. People are confused at first taste, then they become obsessed. The green olives give you what you've been missing in life. If you're basic, leave them out. If you're bold, double them.

64

Side-Eye Dishes

These alpha-gal-friendly stuffed peppers are packed with summer flavor and just the right amount of attitude. Garden tomatoes, gal-free sausage, and a sharp cheddar finish? Don't mind if I do. They're hearty enough for dinner, pretty enough for guests, and just spicy enough to remind the cows that they're not invited.

No Moo, All Boom Stuffed Peppers

Stuffed with garden goodness and zero regrets.
Serves: 4   **Prep Time:** 15 min   **Cook Time:** 35 min
Mood: What am I going to do with all these peppers?
Tastes: Homegrown, hearty, and satisfying, like your garden was an overachiever.

Ingredients
- 4 large bell peppers (tops removed, seeds scooped)
- 1 lb alpha-gal-safe pork sausage
- 2 cups diced tomatoes
- 1 cup cooked rice
- 1 small onion, finely chopped
- 2 cloves garlic, minced
- 1 tsp salt
- 1/2 tsp pepper
- 1 tsp dried basil (or fresh if you fancy)
- 1 cup sharp cheddar cheese (or any alpha-gal-safe brand if you can't tolerate dairy)

Instructions
1. Preheat oven to 375°F.
2. Brown the sausage in a skillet with onion and garlic. Drain if needed.
3. Add tomatoes, rice, salt, pepper, and basil. Stir it up like you're on a cooking show.
4. Spoon the filling into the peppers, packing them as full as a toddler's pockets.
5. Top with a generous handful of cheddar cheese.
6. Bake uncovered for 30–35 minutes, until the peppers are soft and the cheese is golden and smug.
7. Serve hot, along with a side of cucumber salad if your garden's gone rogue.

Note: I love gardening and try to use up everything that grows as you may have noticed.

Sweet Treats

Desserts so good you'll forget ticks ever existed.

68

Sweet Treats

Peaches & Cream & Bacon, Oh My!

Serves: 4   **Prep Time:** 10 min   **Cook Time:** 15 min

Ingredients
- 1/2 block cream cheese, softened
- 4 large ripe peaches, halved and pitted
- 4 oz cream cheese
- 3–4 strips duck bacon, cooked and crumbled
- 1 tbsp honey
- 2 sprigs rosemary
- Olive oil spray

Instructions
1. Preheat oven to 400°F.
2. Lightly oil a baking dish and arrange peaches cut side up.
3. Fill each peach center with cream cheese and top with crumbled duck bacon.
4. Drizzle with honey and lay a rosemary sprig across the top so you'll seem sophisticated.
5. Roast 12–15 minutes, until the peaches are tender and the cheese is golden at the edges. Serve immediately with extra honey drizzle.

Note: These are divine and you're eating fruit, so it must be good for you.

Baked Pears with the Blues

Serves: 4   **Prep Time:** 10 min   **Cook Time:** 20 min
Mood: Fancy.

Ingredients
- 2 ripe pears, halved and cored
- 2 tbsp butter, melted (butter substitute if you can't tolerate dairy)
- 2 tbsp honey
- ¼ cup crumbled blue cheese
- ¼ cup pecans or walnuts
- Fresh rosemary or thyme for garnish
- Optional: Pinch of cinnamon

Instructions
1. Preheat oven to 375°F.
2. Arrange pear halves cut side up in a small baking dish. Brush with melted butter and drizzle with honey.
3. Bake for 15 minutes, until tender but not mushy.
4. Remove from oven and sprinkle with blue cheese and nuts. Return to oven for 5 minutes to melt the cheese slightly.
5. Garnish with fresh herbs and a dusting of cinnamon if desired.

Serve warm.

Note: This dish is classy enough for company but easy enough for Tuesday night. It's also perfect for dessert. Whenever you make it, your mother-in-law will be impressed.

Cheddar Be Good: A Walnut-Pear Love Story

I didn't set out to make a pie until my neighbor gave me five gallons of pears and I ran out of ideas. I made this recipe up and it turned out so good, I'm sharing it with you.

Serves: 8 **Prep Time:** 20 min **Cook Time:** 45 min
Mood: I really need to use up all these pears.
Tastes: Warm, cozy and a little flirty, like blue-ribbon pie-contest-winner vibes.

Ingredients

- 2 store-bought pie crusts thawed (or make grandma proud and sift some flour)
- 6–8 cups sliced ripe pears, peeled
- ½ to ¾ cup sugar (depends how sweet your pears are)
- 2 tbsp butter if tolerated, otherwise oil or duck fat will do
- 1–2 tsp cinnamon
- ½ tsp nutmeg
- 1 tbsp lemon juice
- 1 tsp vanilla extract
- ½ cup chopped walnuts
- ½ to 1 cup sharp cheddar cheese, grated (cheese alternative if you can't tolerate dairy)
- Optional: 1 egg (for egg wash)

Drizzle Glaze
- ½ cup powdered sugar
- 1–2 tsp milk, water, or lemon juice
- Dash of vanilla or cinnamon if you're feeling spicy

Instructions

1. **Prep for Success:** Preheat oven to 375°F. Lay a crust into your pie dish like you do this all the time.
2. **Cheddar the Crust:** Sprinkle a small handful of sharp cheddar over the bottom crust like it's a love letter to your taste buds.
3. **Make the Filling:** In a large skillet, combine pears, sugar, butter, cinnamon, nutmeg, lemon juice, and vanilla. Cook over medium heat until the pears soften and everything gets syrupy and cozy. It'll take about 10–15 minutes.
4. **Add the Walnuts:** Stir 'em in once everything's warm and gooey. They'll toast just enough in the oven for that perfect crunch.
5. **Fill 'er Up:** Pour the pear-walnut goodness into your cheddar-crusted base.
6. **Top Crust On:** Lay the second crust over, crimp the edges like you mean it, and cut a few slits to let it breathe. Brush with egg wash if you want that golden pie flex. I add aluminum foil around the crust edges to prevent burning, but you can now buy pie crust shields. I'm gonna get me one if this book does well.
7. **Bake It Up:** Bake for 45–55 minutes 'til the top's golden brown and the filling bubbles like hot gossip.
8. **Top It Off:** Mix up your drizzle glaze. Start with ½ cup powdered sugar and add liquid slowly until it's pourable but not watery. Once the pie cools slightly, drizzle your glaze on top like you're fancy.

Note: You'll want to serve this up warm with a smug smile. If you're feeling decadent, add a scoop of vanilla ice cream or your non-dairy alternative of choice.

www.ingramcontent.com/pod-product-compliance
Lightning Source LLC
LaVergne TN
LVHW070438070526
838199LV00036B/664